THE
SMART
STARTUP

HOW TO CRUSH IT WITHOUT FALLING INTO THE VENTURE CAPITAL TRAP

BY: JOHN ELDER
StartupFool.com

THE SMART STARTUP

How To Crush It Without Falling Into The Venture Capital Trap

By John Elder

Published By StartupFool.com

CHICAGO, IL USA

ISBN 069246512X

First Edition

Copyright © John Elder
http://www.StartupFool.com

DISCLAMER

All material contained in this book is for informational purposes only and is no substitute for professional advice. Neither John Elder, StartupFool.com or it's affiliates (collectively referred to as COMPANY) make any guarantees of the tactics or strategies described in this book. Successful use of any tactic or strategy described in this book depends on the specific person, their experience, and their business and marketing ability. COMPANY makes no claims or guarantees regarding income generated from the use of any tactic or strategy described in this book. Reader agrees to indemnify and hold COMPANY harmless from and against any and all claims, demands, liabilities, expenses, losses, damages, attorney fees arising from any and all claims and lawsuits for libel, slander, copyright, and trademark violation as well as all other claims resulting from reading this book.

StartupFool.com

For Theresa

TABLE OF CONTENTS

CHAPTER ONE

* * *

INTRODUCTION

So you have an idea for a cool new startup...

These days, it's all about finding the right co-founder, getting into the right tech incubator, raising that first successful round of funding from the venture capitalists, and then totally crushing it.

But that path is wrong...dead wrong.

That old formula might work for some people; but it probably won't work for you and here's the cold hard truth...

If you *need* a co-founder; you aren't going to be successful.

If you *need* to get into a tech incubator to help build out your product; you aren't going to be successful.

If you *need* to raise a ton of money from venture capitalists in order to get your initial product up and running; you aren't going to be successful.

Let those three statements sink in for a minute.

I know you don't want to hear this, but if you really need any of those things to be successful, then you probably don't have what it takes to make it as an entrepreneur.

Instead, you're just some poser wannabe who's bought into the whole startup culture fanboy bullshit myth that's very *very* popular right now.

It's not your fault!

Everyone, and I mean *everyone*, has bought into that myth. Hell, there's even a hilarious HBO series about it called Silicon Valley (have you seen it? It's great!).

They say that the best way to know that a bubble is about to burst is when they make a comedy series about it...

Fortunately, there's a better way, an easier way; one that nearly guarantees your success without costing a fortune or forcing you to give up control to some venture capital douche bags.

I call it the "Smart Startup" and I'm going to teach you how to do it today in this book.

When you build a Smart Startup, you keep 100% of the equity for yourself.

There's no need to share it with a co-founder or give it away to venture capitalists. The point of starting your own company is independence and freedom.

What's the point of building a company when you're at the mercy of a board of directors that was put in place by your VC investors?

Guess what; if you have to answer to someone else – then you're not in charge of anything.

When you build a Smart Startup, you don't have to invest much, if any, capital. I'll teach you how to get a prototype product or service out for pennies (or sometimes free if you can swing a little crowdfunding) and start building honest to goodness sales by growth hacking your marketing for free, immediately.

You'll invest early profits back into the company to help roll out more features and increase market share (as well as hire more technical help without needing to give them equity).

Since you haven't invested much (if any) money, you are free to fail fast and often until you get it right.

Once you *do* get it right, I'll teach you how to scale fast.

This guarantees your eventual success if you just stick with it (and you CAN stick with it because it doesn't really cost you any money every time you fail).

This is a completely different way of looking at things that successful entrepreneurs have known forever and poser wannabe's never seem to get.

When you build a Smart Startup, you'll answer to no one but yourself and your customers. You'll work from anywhere in the world, set your own hours, kick ass in your own way...

...and you'll laugh at all those wannabe posers still following the Venture Capital path to failure.

CHAPTER TWO

* * *

BUSTING THE MYTH

Before we move into the meat and potatoes of the Smart Startup Method, I want to take a few more moments to debunk those first three statements from the beginning of the book.

Why? Because grasshopper, I know that you didn't really believe me when I said that you don't need a cofounder, an incubator, or venture capital to start a company these days.

It's ok, you can admit it – you're skeptical.

You should be!

So let's talk about co-founders. What's so bad about having a cofounder?

The logic seems pretty straight forward. Startups are supposed to have one founder who's good at business stuff, and one who's good at technical stuff.

Seems solid, right?

Sure, on its face, it might make sense to break things down into those two categories. Especially if you're a business or sales oriented person and don't have any tech skills; or a tech minded person who doesn't have any business skills.

But it's a recipe for disaster on many different levels and the truth of the matter is that you can always hire someone to make up for any skills you lack.

An employee that you can fire if things get weird is always better than a partner who you can't fire and who you have to share 50% of all the business profits with forever.

How many startups have crashed because of eventual personality clashes between partners? Gazillions, that's how many.

Listen, startups can be hectic. You're working out of questionable office space (if you have office space at all!), you're working all hours of the day and night, and you probably aren't eating well or getting enough exercise.

It's a recipe for disaster...

Shit happens, tempers flare. Being in a position where you could lose everything over a temper tantrum is not a situation I'd ever want to find myself in.

An employee that pisses you off can be fired immediately. Drop in a new one and carry on.

But let's say you're different. You and your co-founder are best friends, you know that things will never get weird.

Ok fine. That may even be true...

But that still puts you in a position where you have to share 50% of your profits with someone else; forever.

Why do that?

Why pour out the blood sweat and tears needed to build something from scratch; only to share the profits with someone else?

Why?

I don't know about you, but I want to keep all the money. I don't want to share it with a co-founder, and I don't want to share it with a group of venture capitalists. I want it all.

Guess what... I can keep it all if I want to; all I have to do is not have a co-founder.

Amazing!

Listen, I get it. We're not all good at all things. You may think that you really need help in some areas.

But hire what you need! It's so much better for every reason.

I can see the wheels spinning in your mind right now. You still haven't bought in yet...

"But", you ask; "How can I hire talented people if I have no money and don't raise any from venture capitalists?"

That's a good question.

The answer is; initially you aren't going to hire anyone. You're going to learn the skills yourself.

There are really only a handful of skills that you'll truly need to start just about any kind of company, and I'm going to teach you those skills in this book (or point you to great free resources that will teach you).

Don't freak out on me, it isn't going to be that bad.

You'll need to know a few organizational business skills (how to legally form a company, open bank accounts, accept credit cards, keep track of expenses and income).

No problem.

Those are pretty easy things to wrap your brain around and I'll discuss them later on in the book.

Next, you'll need some basic tech skills.

This one is a little harder but not really, and this actually IS one of the areas where you can hire some help *VERY* cheaply if you need it.

I'll show you how later in the book.

Even if you have no tech skills – you should really learn some. It's just stupid not to in this day and age.

I don't know anything at all about septic tanks (those tanks under your house that hold the shit from your toilet).

I can't imagine, in a million years, starting a septic tank cleaning business. Why would I? I don't know a thing about them.

But if I really had my heart set on starting a septic tank business, guess what the very first thing I would do is...

I'd learn everything there is to know about freaking septic tanks!

For some reason though, when it comes to tech startups, people think it's just fine to not have a basic grasp of coding or how the Internet works.

Why would anyone think it's ok to start a tech startup without learning at least a few basic tech skills?

You don't have to know enough to become an engineer. You don't have to know enough to build the next Facebook.

But you should know enough to understand the basics of the Internet.

Things like how web sites are built, a little HTML and CSS, some web hosting basics...things like that.

And that stuff is pretty easy to learn. It'll pay dividends in the future. We'll talk more about this later on.

Finally, you have to know a little about marketing. This is probably the most important skill for you to learn.

You can build the coolest widget in the world, but if you don't know how to sell the damn thing, you won't make any money.

When it comes to sales and marketing, you basically need to bone up on a couple of different things; namely Copywriting and Growth Hacking.

Copywriting is the art and science of selling through the written word. Think sales letters.

It's about writing words that convince people to buy your crap.

These days Copywriting can take many different forms, but when you get right down to it – it's all just copywriting.

It can be the text on your website, or the script for the video that runs on your site (or youtube or wherever), or the sales letter that you email out to your list, or the blog post you make, or the guest article you post on someone else's blog, or the Tweet you send, or the post you make on Facebook.

It's all Copywriting.

All sales eventually come from something you write somewhere, in some form.

There's a right way and a wrong way to do it, and it's something you need to learn.

Learning how to convince people to do things with the power of your pen (so to speak) is a skill that you will use for the rest of your life in a gazillion different ways.

The other marketing skill you need to learn is Growth Hacking.

Growth Hacking entails many different things, but basically it's the art of spreading the word about your products virally.

It's about getting others to tell others who tell others...all at no cost to you.

We're working on a shoestring budget here; we need to focus on marketing methods that don't cost us anything. That's what Growth Hacking is all about.

We'll spend a lot of time on Growth Hacking later on in the book.

That's about it really.

There's nothing too terribly revolutionary about any of those skills. There's nothing you can't learn without a little effort.

And let's face it; if you aren't willing to put forth the effort to learn those things then you don't deserve to play in the NBA. Go back to your stupid boring day job.

My point is; you need these skills regardless...and there's just no need to farm them out by way of bringing in a co-founder.

You'll be stronger in the end if you incorporate these skills into your personal toolbox.

Besides, guess who gets pushed out of a company first in any type of power struggle; the co-founder who understands the nuts and bolts of the business or the one who doesn't?

And that's that.

Now, if you don't need a co-founder because you've taken the time to learn all the skills you'll need to start and run the company yourself, then it follows that you don't need to take money from a VC or get tied up in some incubator.

I'm going to teach you how to churn out your startup fast, how to bring your product to market quickly and with very little money, and finally how to growth hack the hell out of this thing so that sales fly in right away.

You won't need money from VC's to do any of those things.

So why would you give up control of your company, your destiny, your future - to some suit from a venture capital firm?

If your idea is good enough, it will work without needing to throw tons of money at it. A little elbow grease is all it takes.

And if your idea sucks, then no amount of venture capital money will make it work.

People forget that starting a business is all about one thing; and one thing only.

Solving a problem that people have.

If you can solve some problem that people are desperate to solve, then the people will come to you, the sales will come to you; and word of mouth will carry the day in your favor.

And you can't buy that with VC dollars, or a co-founder, or an incubator.

CHAPTER THREE

* * *

THE SMART STARTUP STRATEGY

So what is "The Smart Startup" method?

I've alluded to it already, but now I'll flesh it out in a bit more detail.

We already know that it doesn't involve co-founders, or incubators, or venture capital.

The Smart Startup method is all about starting your business online for little to no money, exploiting Growth Hacking techniques to get the word out and drive initial sales, and then reinvesting profits back into the business to expand and grow (by building out more functionality of your products as well as building out more traditional marketing methods).

On its face, the Smart Startup method may feel a lot like the Lean Startup method developed by Eric Ries back in 2011...but it's not.

Although I've been using the Smart Startup method since 1997, there are some similarities to Lean marketing.

As I understand it, both methods emphasize listening to customers and iterating early based on that feedback. But that's really where the similarities end.

The Smart Startup method is all about the "Big Idea". Identifying that Big Idea early is the most important thing.

So what is a Big Idea?

A Big Idea is something that a complete stranger wants to tell you about. It's shareable.

A Big Idea has to have something special, something out of the ordinary...a wow factor that makes you stand apart from the crowd.

A Big Idea has to differentiate you from everyone else in your market.

A Big Idea has to have a Hook; something that grabs the imagination, or is interesting in some way that is noteworthy.

There is no hard and fast rule that defines a Big Idea. It's one of those things that you know when you see.

It grabs you.

It gets people talking.

When people are talking about your product, you're halfway to your goal. Growth Hacking is all about viral marketing, so the key component is that your Big Idea has to make people want to talk about it.

A *good* idea is not necessarily a *Big Idea*.

For instance, if you can create a widget that works slightly faster than the other widgets in the same market...that might be a Good Idea.

But is that enough to excite people and get them talking about your product? Probably not.

There's no hook, no excitement, no X factor.

With a Good Idea, you can definitely build a business. But you'll never be able to take anything but tiny steps towards your goal. It'll be expensive and wrought with the potential for failure.

A Big Idea, on the other hand, sells itself. It spreads itself virally.

These days, you don't even need a finished product; just the idea of the product can be enough if it comes with a Big Idea.

What do I mean? Look at KickStarter and all the other Crowd Funding sites. People have raised millions of dollars in pre-sales on those sites without ever even creating a product.

Why? Because they were able to ignite people's imaginations with their Big Idea.

Big Ideas sell themselves.

You can pour limitless Venture Capital money into advertising a good idea. Maybe your ads will be successful, maybe they won't.

A Big Idea doesn't require tons of Ad spending, so it doesn't require Venture Capital money.

A Big Idea doesn't require a fancy and expensive website. A simple Wordpress landing page will probably do the trick.

A Big Idea doesn't require spending lots of money to build. You can crowd-fund preorders for your product without giving away equity.

As I understand it, Lean Startups build a simple product and then test the market, get feedback, and change the product based on the feedback (iterate and possibly pivot).

With a Smart Startup, you don't even necessarily need to build the product to get the feedback.

It's all driven by the Big Idea.

Now, a Big Idea doesn't have to be physically big. I'm not saying your idea has to be epic in scale... I'm not talking about building the next Facebook or anything gigantic like that.

And it doesn't have to be spectacular or fantastical, like inventing the hoverboard or x-ray glasses or anything like that.

A Big Idea is about the IDEA, not the size. The Idea has to catch the imagination of the customers.

It just has to have a hook, something that appeals to a market of people, something different enough from what's out there that it gets people talking.

Maybe your Big Idea pisses some people off. Maybe it goes against what people generally believe is the common convention. Maybe it disrupts an established business.

So long as it gets people talking and fills a definite need in a market; you can't go wrong.

So How Do You Come Up With A Big Idea?

Well, that's the hard part and unfortunately I can't answer that.

Only you can come up with your own Big Idea. Only you know your market. Only you know what your potential customers want.

If you don't know what they want, then the very first thing for you to do is *learn* what they want.

Hang out on forums in your industry, sign up for blogs and newsletters in your market, read everything you can, go to conferences, get involved.

If you care enough about a particular market to roll the dice and put your life on the line by starting your own business then by god you should know everything there is to know about the people who buy the products in your field.

How To Know If You've Got A Big Idea?

There are many ways. The easiest answer (and it'll sound like a cop-out) is to float your Idea to your market using some of the Growth Hacking techniques that I'll discuss later in the book and see what happens.

Throw up a landing page asking for the email addresses of people who are interested in your product with a promise to notify them the second the product is released.

Do you get a flood of email addresses? By flood I mean hundreds to thousands. If so you've got a Big Idea.

If not, then you don't.

Ultimately you won't know whether your idea is a Big Idea until you validate it this way.

There are ways that you can help convince yourself that your idea is a Big Idea before you unleash it on the world.

Ask yourself these questions:

- Does This Fill A Real Need In The Market

- Is This Dramatically Different than everything else out there today?

- Is this Disruptive?

- Will This Get People Talking?

- Will It Piss Off Established Players?

- Is It Wholly Unique Or Merely A Small Tweak On Something Already Out There.

- Does It Have A Hook?

- Is The Hook Shareable?

- Will I Need To Throw Ad Dollars At This To Get Traction?

Is your idea big enough that people will come to "know you" for that idea?

Oh that's John, he's the guy who came up with that Smart Startup thing that turned the tech industry on its head.

Oh that's Stacy, she's the one who did that one thing.

Oh that's Bob, you know Bob, he started that such and such thing that everyone's talking about.

A Big Idea is just that. It's identifiable, it's unique, it's shareable, and it can take on a life of it's on with very little effort on your part.

It's not easy.

It shouldn't be easy.

Coming up with your Big Idea is the hardest part of the Smart Startup method.

But trust me, you'll know it when you come up with it. Big Ideas come during "AHA!" moments.

You might be in the shower, you might be walking the dog, you might be watching tv or eating a sandwich... that's when the inspiration for a Big Idea usually hits.

You can't push these things. It's a creative process and it's different for everyone.

The best you can do is learn everything there is to know about your particular market or industry; what products are already out there, what people are looking for, what problems need solving... and then just step back and let all that information gel in your mind.

Walk away from your desk. Wander in the park. Put your mind on anything else and let your subconscious do its job.

When you finally come up with your Big Idea, the next thing to do is act.

You'll need to have a website infrastructure in place, Growth Hacking techniques in place, and the courage to set everything in motion. We'll talk about each of these steps in the next chapters.

CHAPTER FOUR

*** * ***

BUILDING YOUR WEBSITE

No matter what your business is ultimately focused on, no matter what product or service you plan to create, no matter what you want to do; you're going to need a website.

Like I said in the last chapter, you'll need to learn how to do this yourself...at least partly.

You can hire people to build you a website very cheaply, but you still need to know what's involved, and you still need to know the things to tell them to do...if only so that they don't rip you off and over-charge you.

The more you know about building a website, the more you can participate yourself; and the cheaper it will ultimately be.

Let me give you an example of what I'm talking about.

You don't have to be a graphic design expert, or an expert coder. But if you know where to find good Html or Wordpress templates, then you can send your chosen template to someone at elance.com or any of a dozen other freelance sites and tell them "use this template, modify it to do this this and this".

Template tweaking can be done for next to nothing (cost wise). Compared to building something from scratch, we're looking at a difference of thousands of dollars.

And these days, everyone uses templates. Everyone uses common CSS frameworks like Bootstrap.

There's no need to reinvent the wheel.

If you have a basic understanding of how templates work, and a basic understanding of webhosting...you can do most of this stuff on your own.

The only scenario where this doesn't work is if you plan on building the next Facebook, or Twitter, or Pinterest, or Instagram or something massive like that.

In that case, yeah...you won't be able to do it on your own. And you likely won't be able to hire someone to do that cheaply.

But most people shouldn't try to make the next Facebook. If you don't already know how to do something on that large a scale, then you shouldn't be doing it anyway.

Most people looking to start a business have an idea for a product or service. They identify some need that hasn't been met by someone else and they step in to fill that need.

For those people (who are the vast majority of *real* entrepreneurs out there), a simple website based on a simple HTML or a Wordpress template is going to be more than enough to get them off the ground and running.

So that's what I'm going to focus on teaching you.

With just a few basic concepts, you'll be able to throw up a very professional looking website that does absolutely everything you need for next to nothing.

How much is next to nothing?

A really good, top of the line expensive Wordpress theme will cost between $50 and $100. (I've never paid more than like $60 bucks for a Wordpress theme). That's it.

Simple webhosting to get you started can be had for $20-$25 a month and can be operated with ZERO programming knowledge (it's all point, click, and done).

Sure, cheap webhosting isn't going to work for you if you're getting millions of visitors to your website daily...but most of you aren't going to be getting millions of visitors to your website daily; not even hundreds – at least not in the beginning.

We will get into webhosting in a bit; right now I just want to put you into a mindset where you don't have to spend a lot of money to get a professional website.

So first let's define some terms that you're going to run up against in the world of web development.

These will help you to understand the different areas of web development.

You don't necessarily need to learn everything there is to know about these things, but understanding the gist of them is going to help you now; and especially later on when your company expands and you need to start hiring tech people.

So let's talk terms...

Frontend Developer

Backend Developer

Sys Administrators / Devops

Wordpress

Frontend Developer

A frontend developer is someone who focuses on the look and feel of a website. In coder-land, these are people who tend to be less coders, and more graphic design oriented.

That's not to say that they aren't coders too...they are. A good frontend person will know HTML, CSS, and usually Javascript or PHP.

But generally, they're using HTML, CSS, and Javascript/PHP to tweak the look and feel of a site (hence the graphic design designation).

A good frontend person can write code, but also knows their way around Photoshop.

If you want someone who can tweak the look and feel of a Wordpress template, then you're looking for a frontend dev type person with some PHP experience (because Wordpress is built on PHP – more about this later).

There are some frontend people who only focus on coding HTML, CSS, and Javascript.

There are others who only focus on graphic design, photoshop, wire framing, and user experience (UX).

Many have a blend of all those skills.

Backend Developer

A backend developer is typically someone who spends most of their time writing code. These tend to be people with computer science (CS) or engineering degrees.

They aren't tweaking a little HTML or Javascript (though they probably could without much effort), they're building the internal guts of a thing.

Backend developers are usually engineers.

If you WERE building the next Facebook or Twitter, you'd need a lot of backend developers.

If you're just building a basic website to showcase and sell your product or service, you'll almost never need a backend developer.

There are nearly infinite varieties of backend developers, depending on what you need and what computer language you're focused on.

The reason for this is that most backend developers tend to focus on a single computer language (or a handful) and specialize.

You've got PHP coders, Python coders, Ruby on Rails coders, Visual Studio type coders, Database coders, and on and on and on. Not to mention coders who focus on mobile apps (android and apple).

Confused?

Think of it like this...someone who tweaks the look and feel of a Wordpress template is a frontend developer. The people who BUILT Wordpress are backend developers.

Like I said, when it comes to building a simple business website or even a basic ecommerce website, you'll likely never need to deal with backend people.

Sys Administrators / Devops

Systems Administrators and Devops are typically people who run the servers that host the website.

Depending on your system, these people will usually be experts in Linux servers (Or IIS if you're into Microsoft stuff) and things like Apache, Nginx, etc etc.

For basic webhosting, you won't need this kind of firepower. Remember, I said that the kind of webhosting you'll be using in the beginning will all be point and click easy.

But if your business gets bigger, if thousands to millions of people start flooding to your website, then you'll need more serious webhosting power.

These days that means switching over to one of the heavy hitter cloud hosting companies like Amazon AWS or Microsoft Azure.

AWS is not something you can do on your own, it's just too complicated. They're getting better and better over time at making things easier and documenting things better...but they're still light-years away from making it point and click newbie friendly.

You'll need a Sys Admin or Devops type person to set up and maintain a major cloud presence. (Sometimes backend people can handle this if they have those skills).

Don't worry though, by the time you need that sort of firepower, you'll be making more than enough money to be able to afford that type of person. Otherwise, you wouldn't need to migrate to more powerful web hosting solutions.

Wordpress

Finally, let's talk a little about Wordpress. I left it till last, but it's likely to be the most important thing for you to learn about in this chapter.

You probably already know all about Wordpress, heck you might even be running it already for your own personal blog.

Wordpress started out as simple blog software, but has really morphed over time into a full-fledged CMS (content management system).

These days everyone is using Wordpress, not just for blogs, but for the entire range of corporate website needs.

And it's not just people and small companies that are using Wordpress as their main website system; million dollar and even billion dollar companies are using it for their entire online presence.

Why?

Because it's just so easy to use and offers so much flexibility.

Right out of the box, Wordpress just works. With a few clicks of a mouse, you can install a template that's ready to go.

In the space of an hour or two, you can have a professional looking website that does everything you could possibly want it to do, without needing to know how any of it works.

What's more, there's a HUGE ecosystem of plugins (many free or very cheap) that allow you to add some pretty sophisticated functionality with the click of a mouse.

And if you just can't find a point and click solution to your customization needs, it's pretty cheap and easy to hire a freelance coder to make simple tweaks to your wordpress template.

Wordpress allows you to add new content to your site in seconds, and it allows you to change almost anything you want, at any time you want, with the point and click of a mouse.

You don't need an IT department to make changes to your site. You don't need to have your frontend guy write code, and then deploy that code to the backend guy who deploys it to the server. You can do it all yourself in an easy to understand point and click graphical user interface.

Want to add a forum to your website so your customers can ask questions and give feedback? Point and click to install a forum plugin and it's working in seconds.

Want to have a section of the site that customers can log in to and get access to freebies or special offers. There's a dozen plugins that let you do that.

It doesn't matter what you want to do with your website, chances are there's a plugin that will take care of it...and there's a pretty good chance that that plugin will be free or very cheap.

Wordpress levels the playing field and allows anyone to create a professional looking, highly functioning website in seconds.

And Wordpress itself is totally free and usually comes already installed on most web hosts.

You'll pay to buy a custom theme that looks nice (like I said, think $50 - $100 bucks), and you may or may not pay for plugins to add special functionality...but that's about it.

Back at the height of the first dot com boom in the late nineties I started and ran a small web development shop for a while.

Back then people were frantic for websites, and there weren't many people who could build them fast and well.

It was the golden era of the first dot com boom when money flowed like water and talent was pretty hard to come by.

Just to sit down with me and order a website would cost you $20,000. If you wanted something more than a very very *very* basic website, I'd start adding additional fees quickly.

I was so busy that I had to stop taking calls and just ignore new business. People were desperate and even started offering me equity to get me to build their web sites.

These days, you can get a nicer website than what I would have built for you back then, with far far more functionality, all for that $50 that it costs to buy a nice Wordpress theme.

Wordpress evens the playing field tremendously...period.

Static HTML Sites

An alternative to Wordpress is to simply use a static HTML template.

HTML templates don't have any of the functionality of Wordpress, and you'll need to know HTML in order to customize them.

The upside is that they generally run faster (Wordpress comes with a lot of overhead that can eat up bandwidth and take up disk space), and they're also usually a fraction of the price of a Wordpress theme.

Many of the places that sell Wordpress themes will also sell their equivalent HTML template.

So if the Wordpress theme costs $55, then the HTML template might cost $15 or $30 or something like that.

To get an HTML template up and running, you just upload the files to your webhosting account using File Transfer Protocol (FTP) software. Your Web host will give you instructions.

Like I said, you'll need to modify the HTML files yourself in order to customize them. With Wordpress, the themes usually come with some sort of graphical point and click interface that allows you to customize to your heart's content. That isn't the case with an HTML file.

But if you feel confident in your HTML and CSS skills, and don't need any of the added functionality of Wordpress (or any of the plugins), then an HTML template might be right for you.

HTML templates are great for one page websites (or sites with just a few pages).

For instance, if you've got a single landing page that talks about your widget, and at the bottom of the page is a Paypal button that lets people order it...then Wordpress might be overkill and an HTML template might be just fine for you.

Of course, you could still use Wordpress in that situation (and I know many many people who do), I'm just offering you an alternative.

Chances are you'll want to stick with Wordpress.

Where To Find Your Wordpress and HTML Themes

I get asked this one a lot.

There are lots of different places online to find high quality Wordpress and HTML themes. A couple of my favorites are:

http://themeforest.net
http://woothemes.com

Woothemes is a company that produces their own themes. So they have a limited number of Wordpress themes available, but they tend to be pretty good.

ThemeForest.net is more of a marketplace for themes. They have hundreds, maybe even thousands of people who submit their themes for sale on ThemeForest.net

You can browse by category, by popularity, by sales rank, etc and really find the exact theme that you want with the features you need.

They offer both Wordpress themes as well as HTML templates.

Themeforest Wordpress themes tend to run between $50 to $60 bucks, and their HTML templates tend to run between $10 to $30 bucks.

All of the templates and themes listed come with demos so you can see exactly what you're getting before you purchase.

Installing a Wordpress theme is very simple. I could explain it to you but typing out the instructions seems like a waste of time.

I'd much rather just show you with a video (it'll be much quicker and easier to follow that way).

At StartupFool.com I offer a video course that teaches you how to set up a Wordpress site. The course is called "Blog Bootcamp: How To Start A WordPress Blog".

It's normally $49, but as a thank you for purchasing this book, I'd like to give you access for free (we're in this together afterall).

Just head over to:

www.StartupFool.com/wordpress

...and sign up for the course. When you reach the checkout, enter coupon code: smart

That should update the price from $49 down to $0.

The course teaches more than just starting a simple Wordpress blog, it also shows you:

- How to Register a domain name.

- How To Set Up Basic low-cost webhosting

- How to install Wordpress on your webhosting account (if it isn't there already).

- How to install your Wordpress Theme.

- How to find and use Plugins

- How to add posts and pages to your Wordpress Site.

- And much more...

The course is about an hour and a half long and made up of 8 step by step videos where I actually build a simple Wordpress website right in front of you.

Just follow along and do what I do in the videos.

You'll also have access to the comments and questions section underneath each video where you can ask me questions personally.

These days I tend to spend a big chunk of my time lurking at StartupFool.com helping members and answering questions, so chances are; if you post a question I'll answer it within an hour or two.

Not to throw in a shameless plug, but I also recommend that you join StartupFool.com as a full member.

It's not that expensive compared to most IM membership sites out there, and there's just a ton of valuable information and hands on help available for anyone looking to build any type of online business.

Check out StartupFool.com for more details.

We've got tons of step by step videos, daily blog posts, all the books I've ever published on Startups, hands on help, networking and much much more.

END SHAMELESS PLUG

Now let's get back to it.

How Should Your Website Look?

So what should a Smart Startup website look like?

The golden rule is the KISS principle. Keep It Simple Stupid! You don't need to have anything complicated here.

When you have a Big Idea, it's usually pretty easy to articulate that idea. It wouldn't be a Big Idea if it was hard to explain.

So do just that. On the homepage of your site, explain your product or service.

You can use traditional landing page layouts or sales letter type layouts to do this.

It really doesn't matter what your site looks like, because if your idea really is a Big Idea, people will already know what you're selling (because someone they know or trust already told them about it) or they already have a solid understanding from somewhere.

That's part of the beauty of the Big Idea.

In a regular business, you have to spend a decent amount of time convincing people that you're trustworthy and that they should buy the thing you're selling.

With a Big Idea, people tend not to care who you are and won't think twice about handing over their money...they *already want* what you're selling. You just need to throw up a simple website that allows them to order.

Think of it this way...if I found the cure for cancer and started selling it on my website...would anyone care what the website looked like? Would I need to convince them to buy the cure from me? Would they care who I was or what my background is?

Of course not.

Sure, that's a dramatic and slightly hysterical example...but Big Ideas follow that sort of logic.

Here's an example of what I mean...

A few years ago Google changed their algorithm and started penalizing websites that had questionable inbound links.

You see, for years Google ranked websites based on how many links from other sites were pointing to them.

It was sort of like democracy and voting...if 1,000 other websites linked to my website and only 800 sites linked to your website...well then in Google's eyes my website must be better. It has more votes (links) so it would be ranked higher at Google. Higher ranking means more traffic for my website.

SEO people quickly realized this, and so they started building "link farms" to boost rankings.

Link farms are basically just groups of fake websites who only exist to link to other websites.

As more and more SEO types began to use this strategy to game the system, Google search results started getting crappier and crappier.

Finally Google acted.

Almost overnight they started penalizing websites who used these link farms (and other similar methods) to game the system.

So one day your website could be sitting at the top of the search rankings at Google, getting hundreds or even thousands of visitors for free every day; and then the next day your site would disappear from Google completely and your traffic would shrivel up to nothing.

This put a lot of websites out of business, literally over night because people had become dependent on all that free traffic to their website.

Often times the website owners didn't even know they were breaking Google's rules.

People often farm out their SEO work to marketing agencies, and so they had no idea that the marketing agencies were using link farms.

It was bad.

But it was also an opportunity. A friend of mine, I'll call him Tim (not his real name) quickly realized that there was suddenly a market in helping penalized websites get back into Google's good graces.

He also realized that these companies would pay just about anything to fix these problems. I mean, many of those sites were losing hundreds of thousands, if not millions of dollars in revenue from lost traffic.

They'd pay anything to fix that!

Where Tim really shined...and where his Big Idea really took hold...was in offering a 100% money back guarantee.

No one else was doing that. How could they? You couldn't guarantee that Google would let a penalized site back in after they had kicked them out. Sure there were steps you could take, and then you had to stand back, cross your fingers, and hope that Google forgave you...but a guarantee?

Tim didn't care. He decided right then and there to refund anyone's fee if he couldn't reverse their Google penalty.

There were tons of companies offering this exact same service, but no one was offering a guarantee.

People flocked to Tim.

His website was nothing. It was a simple Wordpress landing page that simply explained his service with a few paragraphs, then stated the guarantee and listed a couple testimonials of people who he had helped and who now swore by Tim's service.

As you might expect, Tim's business shot through the roof immediately.

It was literally the next day that orders started pouring in.

He didn't spend much money on advertising, he didn't spend much money on building a fancy website. The Big Idea sold itself.

Profit shot up to just under $130,000 a year and after over five years running it, Tim recently sold that company for $250,000.

Tim was 22 years old when he started that business.

If you can come up with a Big Idea, it's doesn't matter what your site looks like...the Idea will do the selling. It doesn't matter who you are, the Idea will do the selling. It doesn't matter what you spend on adverting, the Idea will do the selling.

So use a standard Wordpress template from Themeforest, or whatever theme marketplace you prefer.

Make a landing page with simple text or a video that explains what you're selling.

Put some sort of order processing form on there (either Paypal, or Stripe, or any of a gazillion other merchant credit card processing systems that usually work out of the box).

Just get something up and move forward.

You can make it look pretty later on when the money starts rolling in.

Video Based Or Text Based Website?

One question I get asked often is whether your homepage should have a video explaining your product, or should you stick with basic text (think traditional sales letter).

The answer is, it doesn't really matter...but I tend to do both when I can.

These days the web is turning more and more towards two things: video and mobile.

Your website should absolutely be mobile ready out of the box.

Don't worry, most Wordpress themes are mobile ready these days so you probably don't have to worry about that (though be sure to check just to make sure before you purchase a theme).

But what about video?

In my opinion, having a simple screenshot video, while certainly not required, helps sell your products.

People prefer to listed or watch someone explain a thing, rather than read about it.

But again, if you have a true Big Idea, it doesn't really matter.

Let me give you a recent example of a site that I built that uses both video and text.

I founded **Codemy.com** at the beginning of 2015 to teach people how to code. The site consists of several courses that people can sign up for to learn different programming languages (mainly Ruby on Rails and PHP).

Take a look at this page:

http://www.codemy.com/rails

That's the sales letter page for my Ruby on Rails course.

The first thing to mention is that this entire website was built using a Wordpress theme that I purchased at ThemeForest.net for (I think) $55.

The second thing to notice is the layout. It's fairly straight forward, there's a menu bar at the top of the screen, followed by a short screencast video that I made (yep that's me talking there).

You can see that there's nothing much to the video, just a series of screencast shots of the course with my voice in the foreground.

I used Camtasia to produce the video very quickly.

The Third thing to notice is that directly below the video I have a more traditional sales letter type layout that gives a little more information about the course, bullet points etc.

Then at the bottom I have an order form button and a couple of testimonials.

There's absolutely nothing special about that web page; but it has a Big Idea.

What's the Big Idea?

Everyone knows there's a gazillion websites out there that teach people to code. Likewise there's a gazillion sites that teach Ruby on Rails.

Hell, there's a gazillion sites that will teach it to you *for free* using videos that are every bit as good as the ones I produced and sell for $97. And let's not even mention Youtube!

But mine video course is different. My Big Idea is basically these two things:

1. I offer hands-on help. The course contains 19 step-by-step videos that actually walk viewers through building a Pinterest type website with Ruby on Rails, but if they have ANY questions at ANY point, they can post them directly under the video and I'll answer them right away. I'll work with them to *MAKE SURE* they understand.

2. I offer a 100% money back guarantee. Students learn to develop websites with Ruby on Rails, the most in demand web development tool out there right now, or they don't pay, period.

It's a powerful selling point, and people understand that right away because Ruby on Rails is really tricky to learn on your own. It's just complicated.

But it gets tremendously easier if you have someone to answer questions. And so that's what I do.

You wouldn't believe how many people tell me that they tried other courses and read other books but got completely stuck along the way; and how my course made it so easy because after I explained a thing, it was as if the answer was obvious – they just needed a little hint, a nudge to get them over that hump.

And guess what... they brag about it to their friends! It's a story they can tell; they're proud of it. "I finally figured out Ruby on Rails – I get it now!"

Big Ideas sell themselves, get people talking, and do your job for you.

The course sells for $97. I released it in January and by April over 1,200 students have taken it. So far only one person has asked for a refund.

If you have a Big Idea, it doesn't matter what your website looks like.

Throw up a video explaining the Big Idea, or throw up a sales letter explaining the Big Idea.

The Big Idea will do the rest.

What About Domain Names?

Domain names tend to freak people out a bit.

Conventional wisdom tells us that there are no good domain names left...all the good ones have been taken.

I don't believe that at all.

Sure, it can be hard to grab the exact domain name that you want; but with a little creativity you should be able to find something that works just fine.

I'll talk about this in a moment. First I want to discuss the different TLD's (top level domains).

The major TLD's are:

.com

.net

.org

.edu

.gov

The rest are generally country specific domains like .co.uk (Britain), .au (Australia), etc.

Then there are other country specific domain names (.co Columbia, .io Indian Ocean) that are popular to use anyway.

For instance, a lot of tech websites like to use .io because they pretend that it stands for input/output and it seems cool.

The rule of thumb when it comes to domain names is that you really need to stick with .com

Many times the specific .com address you want is already taken but the .net or .org is available. It can be really tempting to grab that .net or .org but I suggest you don't do that.

People; regular people - the people who are going to be your customers – they understand .com they know that .com is a website.

It's just more professional, it's what people expect.

So even if you have to jump through hoops to get a .com address that maybe wasn't your first choice (or 100th choice), go with the .com

These days there's a thriving business in selling domain names, and I could write a book about negotiating and buying domain names (I've both bought and sold domain names extensively in the past).

Don't fall in love with a domain name and spend a fortune purchasing it from someone who already owns it.

Spending tons of money (even a couple thousand dollars) on a domain name goes against the whole idea of the Smart Startup.

Because at the end of the day, it's still all about your Big Idea, and a Big Idea doesn't need a fancy domain name.

Try to keep the domain name as small as possible. You don't want something like:

myreallycoolnewblueproduct.com

That's just confusing. Try to be as descriptive as possible yet as small as possible. One or two words...three at the absolute max (if they're small words).

Avoid hyphens at all cost. Take my website, StartupFool.com I would never use Startup-Fool.com

Sure you're going to be tempted to use the hyphen domain name because there are many of them available. There's a reason why they're so much more available; that reason is that they suck...especially for our purposes.

Why?

Because Big Ideas are viral, they get spread by word of mouth. You don't want to make it HARDER for people to tell their friends about your website. Hyphens make it harder.

Give it a try, pretend you're telling a friend about my StartupFool.com website (and pretend it's actually the hyphenated Startup-Fool.com).

"Dude, you've got to check out this website I found, it teaches you how to build an online business for pennies and with like no risk. It's cool, there's all these free videos and tutorials, you can ask questions and get help; it's great! Check it out at Startup hyphen Fool dot com. No you know, hyphen...like a dash. No the big dash in the middle, not the little underscore dash thing. Yeah Startup dash fool.com it's like two words, yeah."

And then imagine the friend, later, trying to remember it. She's going to type in StartupFool.com and probably totally forget the hypen.

It's just a pain in the ass.

So stay away from hyphens in domain names, and stick with .com

Keep it as short as possible; keep it as memorable as possible. The truth of the matter is that most people aren't going to type in the URL of your website into their web browser. People just don't do that anymore.

Instead they search for it at Google and click the link, or click a link on Facebook or Twitter etc.

So in the ultimate sense, it really doesn't matter what your domain name is. But you might as well stick with the best practices I just laid out for you if at all possible. Just in case...

What Do Domain Names Cost?

Domain names generally cost around $10 per year. You sort of rent them in the sense that you own them for as long as you continue to pay the yearly fee (of around $10 depending on the registrar you use).

If you stop paying the yearly fee, you no longer own the domain name.

So in a sense you do and you don't own a domain name.

There are lots of different registrars where you can register your domain name. Some are good, some are bad, and all of them charge different prices.

I tend to use NameCheap.com for all my domains. They're cheap and they don't give you any bullshit like other registrars do.

GoDaddy.com is another registrar that I'll use from time to time because they often run promotions where you can register a domain name for $.99 cents on up to $5.99 depending on the particular promotion.

Always search for coupon codes when you use Godaddy.

When I do use Godaddy.com, I tend to transfer my domain name to NameCheap.com after the first year because I find that Godaddy tends to charge too much for subsequent year registration fees.

Sure you might get that domain name for $.99 cents for the first year, but then Godaddy might jack up the price to $14.99 or more for the next year and the next year and the next year etc.

So when my first year is up, I always transfer the domain to my NameCheap account. This is quick, easy, and free to do (you just have to pay the next yearly fee at NameCheap.com at the time of the transfer).

Sure, if Godaddy charges $14.99 for that second year, and NameCheap.com charges $9.99 for the second year, I'm only saving like $5 bucks...and that's not much money...it might be a moot point.

Personally, I own hundreds... sometimes thousands of domain names so that extra $5 bucks adds up for me in a hurry. If you just have one or two domain names, it might not matter to you.

You do sort of have to worry about Godaddy because they will smother you with bullshit.

They'll try to upsell you all kinds of weird services that you don't need or wouldn't want and they make their checkout process as confusing as possible in order to trick you into agreeing to pay for those upsell items. Just be careful.

I've also had Godaddy do underhanded things to me in the past. Whenever I order a domain name from them, I immediately turn OFF the auto-renew option.

Auto-renew is the option to have them automatically charge your credit card a year from now when it's time to renew your domain name... at whatever the current price Godaddy chooses to charge you (which will be more expensive than many other registrars).

You might think...hey, auto-renew is a great idea because that way I won't forget!

Well you won't forget anyway because they send out a steady stream of email reminders whenever you approach a renewal period (because they want you to renew so they can charge you). So it's not like you will forget and lose your domain name.

Since I plan on always transferring my domain name away from Godaddy after the first year, I ALWAYS ALWAYS ALWAYS turn off auto-renew.

In fact, I have it set in my preferences to automatically turn off auto-renew for all new domain purchases.

But it never fails...I'll go back in my domain dashboard months after I've purchased a domain name and see that several of my domains mysteriously have auto-renew turned on.

It's not a mistake...I believe that they do that on purpose and other registrars probably do the same.

I don't really blame Godaddy for trying these shenanigans. They pretty much have to in order to offer $.99 domain deals and to pay for all those stupid Godaddy commercials on tv.

Just be aware of it and keep your eyes open. I'm willing to put up with their nonsense in exchange for cheap domains, but you can make up your own mind.

StartupFool.com

CHAPTER FIVE

* * *

BUSINESS STRUCTURES

This is the chapter that no one really wants to read, but you probably should...especially if you don't have any formal business organizational knowledge.

It's going to be dry and boring. Read it anyway. It can save you thousands of dollars, or more.

We've already talked about building your web site, but that might have been putting the horse before the cart a little bit.

Before you build a website or sell a single item, you need to decide on a business structure.

You need to determine what type of business entity you'll be starting, set up bank accounts, set up credit card processing of some sort, create a system to track orders and expense, and all the generally boring crap that no entrepreneur really wants to deal with ever.

Unfortunately those things are important; vitally important.

Now before we go on I have to give you the standard bullshit disclaimer that I am not an attorney or a certified public accountant. Therefore I am in no way qualified to give you any of the advice that I'm about to give you and so you should absolutely not listen to a single word I'm about to say in this chapter.

Instead, you should go out and spend thousands of dollars on an attorney who can advise you and fill out all the proper paperwork and register you for all the local permits and licenses that you need to conduct business in your local, state, and federal area.

That being said, let's break all this down. Everything I talk about in this chapter will be geared towards people living in the United States because that's what I'm familiar with. Other countries have other laws and regulations.

First you need to form a company. You need some entity other than yourself for many different reasons.

Yes, you can just run things in your own name and call yourself "Self-Employed" without forming any sort of business entity, but that's a really bad idea.

Why?

People will sue you. They'll sue you for no real reason whatsoever if they think you have some money.

If it costs $10,000 and three years of your life to successfully defend yourself from a frivolous lawsuit, someone is eventually going to file that lawsuit and offer to settle for $5,000.

That's an over simplification, but you get the idea.

Patent trolls might sue you, competitors might sue you, disgruntled customers might sue you. The list goes on and on.

If there's no actual company to sue, they'll sue you personally. If you have a company, then they will sue the company and your liability could be limited.

Limiting liability is a very good reason to form a company, but it's not the only one.

Depending on the type of company you form, there are all sorts of tax benefits as well. Corporations and Limited Liability Companies get all kinds of neat tax breaks in the form of deductions.

Finally, having your own company is just the professional thing to do. Are you a professional or just some weirdo trying to make a little money?

So form an actual company. Yes, there are costs involved and you'll probably have to do a little research first...but it's well worth the time and energy and I'll try to point you in the right direction.

What Are Your Options?

When it comes to forming a company you have several options. You can form a Corporation (Inc), or you can form a Limited Liability Company (LLC).

You can also form a Partnership but I generally recommend against that so I'm not even going to discuss it (if you do have a partner, you can still form a Corporation or LLC without the need to form a formal Partnership).

Corporations and LLC's are separate legal entities. They are totally independent of you. The law treats them as their own person. That's important to remember because you need to treat them as separate creatures yourself.

That means that you need separate bank accounts from yourself (you can't use your own regular checking account).

It also means that they need to file their own tax returns (Corporations file their own Corporate taxes and LLC's file Schedule SE and Schedule C on your personal tax return).

And it also means that they have to track their own expenses separate from your own normal personal expenses.

Corporations and Limited Liability Companies are very different entities, and you need to understand the difference between them before you decide which one to choose. I'll discuss them a bit in this chapter, but ultimately you should do a little more research on it yourself.

Google is a good place to start, or even one of those "Incorporate Your Business for Dummies" books isn't an entirely bad idea to browse through.

So let's break each of these two options down...

Corporations

Corporations intimidate a lot of people who are just starting out. Apple, Microsoft, Google...these are all corporations. People think "I'm just some chick with an idea I can't be a corporation!"

Anyone can form a corporation.

You don't have to have tons of employees (or any for that matter), you don't have to have fancy offices (or any for that matter), you don't have to do much of anything except fill out the form, mail it to the state agency responsible for business registration in your state, and pay the fee.

But what exactly is a Corporation?

Well, it's a legal entity created to engage in business. And it's a specific entity...meaning that it consists of Shareholders, who elect a Board of Directors, who hire a Management team to run the company.

Don't worry, YOU can be the single shareholder of the Corporation, and as the majority shareholder you can elect yourself to the Board of Directors (congrats, you're the Chairman of the Board now!), and as the sole Board member, you can choose to hire yourself as the Chief Executive Officer (CEO) and Secretary, and Treasurer of the company.

One person can be all of those things.

That's how a Corporation works. You become an employee of the Corporation (it's CEO). The company pays you a salary. The company matches your payroll taxes and files its own corporate tax returns each year.

The company also gets to deduct normal business expenses.

Here's a simplified example to help you get a sense of things.

Let's say that the first year in business your company earns $100,000.

Let's say you paid $10,000 in office rent and utilities, $5,000 in webhosting fees, and $5,000 in other miscellaneous office fees. Let's say that you paid yourself a salary of $80,000.

So we have:

Simple Profit/Loss Satement

Revenue:	$100,000
(minus)	
Expenses	
Rent	($10,000)
Hosting	($ 5,000)
Misc.	($ 5,000)
Salaries	($80,000)
Total Exp.	($100,000)

Total Profit $0

The company earned $100,000 in revenue, but had $100,000 in expenses. So there was zero profit.

Corporations are generally only taxed on their profits...so in this example the corporation would owe ZERO in taxes.

Of course, you personally still have to pay taxes on your salary of $80,000 like you would at any regular job (and the corporation does match your payroll taxes).

The corporation still has to fill out a federal and state tax return and mail them in...but it won't owe state or federal corporate taxes.

The great thing about all this is that Corporations can deduct all sorts of things that you might normally pay for yourself...like cell phone usage, certain mileage on your car, rent (the corp can actually pay you a certain amount of rent if it operates out of your home) and many other things.

Why is that important?

It's important because it will lower your personal tax rate if you can legally shift some of your personal expenses into the corporation.

Having trouble conceptualizing that? Let's try an example. Now, this is just an example to prove the concept; as always – check with a certified public accountant before engaging in ANY tax strategy.

So let's stick with the same numbers as above. The corporation earns $100,000 and pays you $80,000 in salary.

As I mentioned before, the corporation now owes zero in corporate tax, but you still owe regular income tax on the $80,000.

I checked the tax tables at the IRS website, and on $80,000 in salary your tax (assuming you are single) would be $15,863.

So of the $80,000 you pay yourself; $15,863 goes to federal taxes and that leaves you $64,137.

For the sake of simplicity I'm going to ignore state taxes.

Now, let's say every year you like to go on vacation to Aruba, and it usually costs you about $5,000.

So $64,137 – 5,000 = $59,137

Let's just introduce one new expense to the corporate equation...

Every year by law you are required to hold a meeting of the board of directors. You can hold that meeting anywhere you want, and it's a legitimate business expense. Let's say you decide to hold it in Aruba.

Let's say it costs $5,000 to fly your board of directors (ie you) down to Aruba and put you up in a hotel for x days.

Well now the corporation has $5,000 less dollars and so it reduces your salary down to $75,000 (from the $80,000 it was before).

So let's play our game and run the numbers:

Simple Profit/Loss Satement

Revenue:		$100,000
minus		
Expenses		
Rent	($10,000)	
Hosting	($ 5,000)	
Misc.	($ 5,000)	
Salaries	($75,000)	
Meeting	($5,000)	
Total Exp.		($100,000)

Total Profit $0

The corporation still has a total profit of zero, therefore owes no corporate taxes.

You, on the other hand, earned less money...so your tax rate is now lower!

On $75,000 in salary, you'll only pay $14,613 in federal income tax. Remember, when your salary was $80,000 you paid $15,863 (or $1,250 more).

So what are you left with?

$75,000 - $14,613 = $60,387

In scenario one when you paid for your Aruba trip with your own money after taxes, you ended up with $59,137.

In scenario two when you paid for your Aruba trip through the tax deductable corporation, you ended up with $60,387 personally. That's a big savings!

Just by switching one thing, you ended up $1,250 richer.

And there are tons of things like that that you can do as a Corporation.

Get a book on corporate tax deductions and talk to a CPA.

CPA's (certified public accountants) are cheap. Mine charges a couple hundred bucks per year to do my corporate taxes (mainly because my corporate taxes are pretty simple and straight forward), and will usually take a phone call from me to answer a simple deduction question from time to time at no charge.

When you're first starting out, you probably won't have a relationship with a CPA so you'll probably have to pay for that kind of advice.

That's fine, it won't cost much. Ask them how much for a half hour conference. It's probably gonna be a hundred bucks or so (depending on what area of the country you live in...busy CPA's in the city will charge more, rural CPA's in the slow non-tax season will be cheaper).

Ask them what you can legally deduct. Follow the rules.

Paying for things through your corporation before taxes can dramatically lower your taxes.

Many, if not most of the same deductions are available to Limited Liability Companies as well and I'll talk about them in a bit.

Types of Corporations

There are actually a couple of different types of corporations, and you'll have to choose between them. The two main types that we need to worry about are:

C-Corp
and
S-Corp

A C-Corp is the standard Corporation. Normally, when we're talking about corporations, we're talking about C-Corps.

An S-Corp is slightly different.

Remember how I said that a corporation has to pay its own taxes and file its own tax return? Well if you don't plan correctly, this can actually mean that you'll get taxed twice.

Twice? Yep. The Corporation pays taxes, and then you pay taxes on any dividends that the Corporation pays you (more on dividends in a bit).

In our previous example, the corporation owed zero taxes because it had zero profit. But sometimes that might not be the case.

The corporation might have expenses that are NOT deductable.

In our first example, the corporation paid you a salary of $80,000. Salaries are generally only deductable up to the amount of normal salaries for your industry.

So if you own a software company, and CEOs in your industry generally earn between $150,000 and say $300,000 in salary, then that's how much the IRS will let you deduct as a business expense.

What happens if your company earns, say, a million dollars? Let's say we had those same expenses as before (rent of $10,000, webhosting of $5,000 and misc of $5,000 to equal $20,000 of expenses).

Let's say we increased your salary from $80,000 to $300,000. Here's what our profit loss statement would look:

Simple Profit/Loss Satement

Revenue:		$1,000,000
minus		
Expenses		
Rent	($10,000)	
Hosting	($ 5,000)	
Misc.	($ 5,000)	
Salaries	($300,000)	
Total Exp.		($320,000)

Total Profit $680,000

Suddenly the corporation has a profit of $680,000 and will have to pay taxes on it!

Let's say that the corporate tax rate is 30%; that means you're paying $204,000 in taxes and are left with $476,000.

Now what? Well you want that money, right? So to take it out of the corporation you will have to declare a Dividend.

So you pay yourself $476,000 in dividends.

Ah, but guess what...now you owe personal taxes on the Dividend!

Let's say you owe 20% capital gains on the dividend...that's $95,200.

Of the $476,000, you're now left with just $380,800.

That's Double Taxation

This sucks because you've been taxed twice! The corporation paid $204,000 in corporate tax and you paid $95,200 in capital gains tax on the dividend! That's $299,200 in taxes on $680,000 in profit.

Or about 45% in taxes! Whew!

Why can't you just increase your salary to $980,000 and deduct it? Because the IRS doesn't consider that within the average salary of a small software company so won't let you deduct it as a business expense.

Sure, you COULD pay that money to yourself as salary (but then you'd be paying the highest personal income tax rate which is massive) but the IRS would still make you pay corporate taxes on the amount over the $300,000 it lets you deduct as an ordinary business expense.

It's still basically double taxation.

This double taxation thing likely isn't a problem you'll have to deal in the beginning because your company may not make that much money right away.

One way to get around this is with an S-Corp.

S-Corp

An S-Corp behaves similarly to a C-Corp except that it is not taxed itself. Instead, profits and losses pass directly to the shareholders (ie you).

You then list them on your personal tax return.

The S-Corp still has to file a tax return, but owes no taxes (you'll pay all the taxes on your personal return).

As an individual, you'll receive a Schedule K-1 that lists how much money is being distributed to you, and how much expenses the company incurred. You then plug those numbers into your personal tax return.

There are good things and bad things about S-Corps, and it's a little beyond the scope of this book to go into it in any greater detail.

Personally I've never used an S-Corp for lots of reasons, but you can do some research and decide yourself.

Limited Liability Companies

A Limited Liability Company (LLC) is very different from a Corporation, but allows many of the same benefits.

Like a Corporation, an LLC is a separate legal entity, but unlike a C-Corp, all the profits are passed through to the members of the LLC.

In a Corporation you have shareholders, in an LLC you have "members", but they behave similarly.

LLC's are generally called "Pass-Through" entities because profits and losses pass through to the members, very much like with an S-Corp.

There are basically two types of LLC's, "single member" and "multi-member".

With a single member LLC, the profit and loss are passed to you, the single member, and you declare them on your personal tax return using Schedule C and Schedule SE.

Multi-Member LLC's are treated and taxed more like partnerships. They're really a hybrid between a partnership and a corporation (sort of like an S-Corp).

You'll get a K-1 form each year at tax time just like with an S-Corp.

There are lots of benefits to forming an LLC, especially a single member LLC.

You get all of the liability protection that you would with a corporation, but with much less formal nonsense to deal with like paperwork and corporate tax returns to file, and annual shareholder and board meetings to hold.

With corporations there are always yearly fees to pay to the secretary of state, you have to hold and record formal shareholder and board of director meetings every year (even if you are the only shareholder or director), and there's just a lot of paperwork in general to deal with.

Head over to the IRS website and check out Schedule C. That's the form you fill out for your personal taxes with an LLC. It's pretty simple! You just list your income, and your expenses, and bam - you're done.

Then you fill out Schedule SE, which calculates your Self Employment tax (which sort of taxes the place of normal payroll taxes).

It's pretty simple.

LLC's are a relatively new thing. Back when I started building companies in the mid 90's, there wasn't much information on LLC's and they weren't in use all that much.

These days they are ordinary and popular. You get your shielded liability, you can deduct your business expenses, and there's no tedious corporate tax returns and other nonsense paperwork to file every year.

I generally tend to recommend LLC's to people starting a new company, especially if they are just one person.

LLC's costs different amounts of money to form in different states. Every state is different. Some states charge less than a hundred dollars to create an LLC (and one form to fill out). Others charge hundreds, up to $800 or more.

Guess what, you don't necessarily need to form your LLC in the same state that you live in.

Shop around! Find the cheapest and easiest state to form yours in. You just need to hire a "Registered Agent" to receive official mail from the government for your LLC in the state that it is formed.

Registered Agents can be found online for $100 a year or less.

Talk to your CPA before forming any sort of company, in your own state or any state.

CHAPTER SIX

* * *

FORMING YOUR COMPANY

Don't worry; we're almost through the tedious stuff. Now we just need to talk about actually setting up your company.

We've talked about the different types of business entities that you can form, and hopefully I've at least given you enough information to get you started so that you can do a little more research on your own.

I recommend you hit Wikipedia and read the entries for C-Corp, S-Corp, and Limited Liability Companies. Then Google each and read a little more.

Then I suggest that you find a bookstore (if you can still find an actual bookstore somewhere) or a library, and grab a book on the subject.

Look for titles like "How to form a Limited Liability Company" or "Limited Liability Companies for Dummies" if you're steering towards LLCs.

If you're thinking about forming a corporation, look for titles like "How to incorporate and form a company in Illinois" or whatever state you live in.

You don't necessarily need to buy them, but browse through them. They'll discuss things I missed.

How To Form A Company

So how do you actually go about creating one of these things anyway?

Companies are State creatures (both LLC's and Corporations). By that I mean that the State government creates them, not the Federal government.

You won't send in an application to form a business to the Federal government, you'll send it to the State government.

Here's the fun part...each State has different rules, laws, and fees for forming a company. And most states have totally different rules, laws, and fees for corporations and LLC's.

It might cost $300 to form a corporation in State A, and $200 to form an LLC in that same state.

It might cost $800 to form an LLC in State B and $200 to form a corporation in that same State.

It's a bit goofy.

Generally speaking, you're going to want to form your corporation or LLC in the state that you live.

But you don't necessarily have to. If your state makes you jump through insane hoops to form a company (like makes you fill out 10 pages of very complicated forms and licenses etc) and charges you a lot, then look for another state.

Registered Agent

Like I mentioned before, you merely need a Registered Agent in whatever state your company is formed in. The Registered Agent is someone with a physical mailing address in that state who agrees to accept official mail for your company and forward it on to you.

What's the purpose of this? The state needs an official mailing address to send official mail.

And if someone wants to sue you, they need an official address to serve the paperwork to, etc.

You won't use your Registered Agent as your business address for ordinary mail (like to send regular bills and things like that to), they're just for official mail.

YOU can be your own Registered Agent and your house can be the address if you live in the same state that your company is formed in...

But if you're shopping around for a cheaper state, then you'll need to hire a Registered Agent.

Google it. Most incorporation services offer Registered Agent service for around $100 bucks a year.

Incorporation Services

Sure, you can do the research and figure out exactly what forms to fill out and how to fill them out correctly yourself, but for those of you who don't want to do that or don't feel confident that you'll get it right, there are tons of Incorporation Services online that will fill out all the forms and mail them to the appropriate government agency for a fee.

They'll form both Corporations and LLC's.

Usually it'll cost you around $100 to $150 to use those services (plus whatever government fee your state charges to form a company).

Shop around for cheaper prices here, some incorporation services charge more than others and they all provide the same basic services.

They'll try to upsell you things that you don't need...like a fancy leather bound three-ring binder to hold your corporate documents in, etc. You don't need any of that stuff.

The first time I formed a corporation I used an incorporation service...then afterwards I had a copy of all the forms they filled out to start my corporation and realized that I could easily fill out those forms myself now that I knew what to write on them...

So I never used a service after that.

These days I tend to form LLC's for new business ventures, and they can be even easier to create. It's really just up to you.

Usually business formation is handled by a state's "Secretary of State" office. If not, it's usually some standard sounding office like "The Office of Business Services" or something like that.

A Google search for "How to form an LLC in Illinois" or "How to form a corporation in Illinois" or whatever your state happens to be will sort you out in moments.

Generally, for a Corporation, you'll file "Articles of Incorporation" and for an LLC you'll file "Articles of Organization".

Each state requires something different for each of those things.

In Illinois as of the publication of this book, it costs $600 to file Articles of Organization to form an LLC in Illinois; and it costs $281.25 to file Articles of Incorporation to form a Corporation.

Seem weird to you? It is. Usually LLC's are cheaper to form than Corporations because they are far less complicated entities.

But Illinois is ass backwards for some reason.

So I never form an LLC in Illinois (and I've got a bunch of them!)

Its Illinois' loss (thank your politicians). There are states that charge $100 or less to form an LLC and require like one single paged form to do it...

At StartupFool.com, we're working on a pdf that breaks down all the states filing requirements and fees so that you can see at a glance which ones are cheapest and easiest to form your company in.

If it's not quite done yet when this book is published, it will be very soon. You can grab a copy of it for free at:

www.StartupFool.com/inc

If it isn't up yet by the time this book goes to press, I'll slap up a form where you can at least enter your email address and get notified when it's ready.

Tax ID Number

Besides filling out the articles of incorporation or organization with your state, the only other real thing you need to do is grab yourself a Tax Id Number (sometimes called an Employer Identification Number or EIN).

Remember how I said that Corporations and LLC's are creatures of the State? Well, you also need to let the Federal Government know they exist. They need some way to keep track of you for tax purposes, and the EIN is how they do that.

An EIN is sort of like a social security number for your company. You'll need one no matter what type of company you form (corp or LLC).

This number is important for tax reporting purposes, but it's also important for lots of other reasons. You'll use it all the time.

Banks will require it to open bank accounts, Insurance companies will probably want it, etc etc etc.

The EIN is the identification number for your business...much like a social security number identifies you as a person.

Luckily, it's very easy to get an EIN number, and it doesn't costs a thing.

You can do it all online in minutes without ever even talking to a human being.

Back in the day, you actually had to call the IRS and wait on hold half the day to get one of these numbers, but these days it's super easy online.

Form SS-4

To get an EIN you just need to fill out form SS-4 with the IRS, and you can do that online.

Run a Google search for SS-4 and you'll get a link to the IRS website page as well as a link to their instructions page if you don't understand something.

The form is one page long, and a little hard to understand in places if you don't really know what you're doing...so read the instructions if you get confused.

Head over to StartupFool.com if you get stumped and shoot me a message. I'll walk you through it if you need help.

When you search for SS-4 at Google, you'll get links to the form itself as well as the SS-4 info page at the IRS.

You don't want to fill out the actual PDF yourself, instead find the link that says "Apply for an EIN online" or something like that.

The IRS's online application is more like a question and answer walkthrough that then spits out a filled out form and zaps it over to the IRS for you.

You'll get your EIN immediately, print it out and write it down!

PRINT OUT THE NUMBER!

When you complete the application, you'll get a confirmation type form with your new EIN. PRINT THAT OUT!

A lot of banks will want an actual copy of that stupid thing to open checking accounts etc. It's not good enough to just write down the number and give it to them. It's stupid, I know...but they want to see the form.

The IRS website will give you that form to print out and then it'll say something like "And we'll also mail you a copy of this within 10 days" or some shit.

More often than not, it never shows up in the mail. Bureaucracy.

So print it out at the time you apply. Hold on to it, make copies. Save the PDF to dropbox or evernote.

What Else?

Basically that's all there is to it. Depending on your state, it can take a few weeks to a couple of months for them to process your articles of incorporation or organization.

When they do, they'll usually give you a file number that you'll want to hang on to.

Other than that, there may be other requirements depending on your state, county, and even city.

If you plan on running your company out of your home or an office, some cities require that you register through the city or county clerk.

Some states require that you apply for a state business license, and sales tax license.

You'll just have to research your own area to be sure.

The Internet is your friend; you can probably find that info with a quick Google search.

Or you can always hire a local attorney to do ALL of this stuff for you (though that will be expensive).

Local CPA's (certified public accountants) usually know how to fill out all the forms and what's required too...and will usually work much cheaper than an attorney.

It's really just up to you how comfortable you feel doing it yourself, hiring an incorporation service, or using an attorney or CPA.

Next you'll want to open a checking account in the name of your business.

Make sure it's a business checking account, not a personal one. The bank will want your EIN number, maybe your State file number, and possibly a copy of your articles of inc. or org.

Try to find one that doesn't charge you a monthly fee to use basic checking. These days it's harder and harder to find a bank that offers free checking.

Hit the Internet and search for "Free Business Checking" and hit the pavement.

These days you generally can't open a checking account online (though sometimes you can). That means you'll probably have to show up at a bank in person.

It can take a half hour to an hour to set up a checking account these days because they need to make sure you aren't a terrorist. It's fairly ridiculous, but there you go.

Just be sure to bring all your paperwork like your EIN number, your articles of inc or org, and anything else.

A good rule of thumb is to call the bank and ask them exactly what they need by way of paperwork to open an account.

If you're running a corporation, they're probably going to want you to bring a formal written "resolution" from your board of directors authorizing you to open checking accounts.

Search online for sample corporate resolutions that you can print out for free.

A resolution is basically just a few lines on a piece of paper saying "We the board of directors authorize CEO Jane Doe to open checking accounts in the name or the company at XYZ bank".

Then you sign as the chairman of the board and secretary of the company. It's absurd, but banks are absurd; so there you go.

Other than that...you should be good to go!

I know this has been a fairly tedious and boring couple of chapters, but getting this stuff done is fairly important so it's worth it to take the time to learn all you can about it.

In the next chapter we'll start talking about the fun shit...Growth Hacking.

CHAPTER SEVEN

* * *

GROWTH HACKING

It's time to get back to the fun stuff. We've meandered pretty far off the beaten path of the Smart Startup method to talk about forming a business; now it's time to get back to the meat and potatoes of this thing.

So you've formed your company, you've got checking accounts set up so that you can accept money in exchange for your Big Idea product or service, and you've got a basic website set up – probably using wordpress.

Now it's time to start marketing you stuff.

When it comes to Smart Startups and marketing, it all comes down to Growth Hacking.

So what is Growth Hacking?

For the longest time I didn't pay any attention to Growth Hacking. I thought it was just the latest stupid buzzword...and I was right.

When I finally took the time to really learn what this Growth Hacking thing was all about, I realized that it's exactly the kind of marketing that I've always done. I mean always, ever since 1997 when I first dropped out of college to start one of the Internet's earliest online advertising networks.

Back then we didn't call it Growth Hacking, we called it Guerilla Marketing, but it's essentially the same thing.

Guerilla Marketing is the act of marketing using unconventional methods that don't cost any money. Just like guerilla warfare, you use your cleverness instead of your pocketbook.

Guerilla Marketing has morphed over the years into what we now call Growth Hacking because the Internet gives us all kinds of amazing tools that didn't exist back then.

We'll talk about some of those tools... but the tools aren't the important thing to focus on...it's the Guerilla part that's important.

To understand Growth Hacking, you first have to understand traditional marketing; at least a little bit.

Traditional Marketing

Traditional Marketing is very straight forward. You define your market, determine how to reach your market, put your message in front of your market (usually by way of some sort of paid advertising), then track conversions and tweak and test things to convert better (ie re-write your sales copy, shoot a better sales video, etc).

In a nutshell, that's traditional marketing.

You calculate the lifetime value of a customer (how much on average you can expect to earn from a single customers), discount that amount back to present value using basic discounted cash flow (dcf) algebra, and then try to spend less than that amount to acquire each new customer.

For instance, if you know that on average you can expect to earn $500 per customer over a 5 year period, you can discount that $500 to present value dollars and it might end up coming out to..say...$429 bucks.

If you spend on average less than $429 bucks in advertising to acquire each new customer, you've got yourself a successful business.

You know... in a nutshell.

The problem with our Smart Startup is that we don't really know what the value of our customers are going to be over the lifetime of the product line, and we don't really have any money to invest to acquire ANY customers.

So advertising is out.

That means we need to turn to alternative methods of acquiring new customers - Guerilla Warfare type methods.

These methods need to be cheap or, better yet, completely free.

They need to be self-sustaining if possible, meaning once you put them in motion they take on a life of their own.

Finally, they need to be trackable. We need to be able to track them to determine whether or not they are successful.

Luckily, it's never been easier to get the word out about your product or service at no cost.

It's not easy, but it's never been easier...

A Growth Hacking Example

Like I mentioned earlier, Growth Hacking is the latest marketing buzzword, and as such there seems to be lots of people talking about it. They all seem to give the same example of Growth Hacking so I thought I would too.

Remember Hotmail? It was the first really big free webmail email service. These days everyone uses Gmail and we tend to turn our noses up at stodgy old Hotmail, but back in the day it was quite a thing.

Hotmail was founded back in 1996 (The same year I started my Advertising Network) by Sabeer Bhatia and Jack Smith.

Microsoft bought the company about a year later towards the end of 1997 for around $400 million dollars.

Seems like a runaway success, right? If someone gave me $400 million bucks for a company I started a year before, I'd call that an instant success.

But the reality is actually very different.

When the company got bought by Microsoft, they claimed to have between 8.5 and 12 million users, which was a pretty big number back then (there were only about 70 million people using the Internet at the time).

But when the company first started, things didn't go so smoothly...

During their first month, the company only managed to persuade twenty thousand people to sign up.

20,000 people aren't very many.

It was reported that the company had initially raised $300,000 – so they didn't have a lot of money to spend on advertising.

Legend has it that the company was planning to spend their cash on radio and billboard ads.

Fortunately, someone came up with a better idea.

They started putting six little words at the bottom of every email that a user sent out.

The words?

"Get Your Free Email at Hotmail"

(Well, initially it said "PS, I love you, Get Your Free Email at Hotmail" but they quickly dropped the PS I love you part).

Growth shot up instantly. Within the next month, their user base had grown to one million users, and it grew exponentially from there.

Less than a year later the founders were $400 million dollars richer.

Adding a simple tagline to the bottom of every email sent out through their service didn't cost them a penny.

It turned each and every one of their customers into an advocate for the company. The more often people used the service, the more free advertising Hotmail received, resulting in more people using the service, resulting in more free advertising for Hotmail, resulting in, resulting in, resulting in...$400 million dollars.

See what I mean when I say that Growth Hacking feeds into itself?

It builds its own momentum.

Pairing Growth Hacking with a Big Idea is a recipe for achieving a high probability of success. It's powerful stuff.

How To Come Up With Your Own Growth Hack

The Hotmail example is a great example; that's probably why everyone uses it to define Growth Hacking.

But it probably doesn't apply to you unless you're building some sort of online service.

Hell, it might not apply at all these days because we've become inundated by advertising – we're numb to it.

How many services offer a free tier with advertising? Tons. We've learned to ignore that kind of advertising.

So I'm skeptical that something like this would even work today.

It's the *idea* behind that particular growth hack that's important.

It's the idea of taking a look at what you have, and tweaking it to take advantage of the situation.

Unfortunately I can't tell you "Do this, this, and this" and you'll be successful. You need to invent your own Growth Hack.

Sure there are some basic Growth Hacking tips and tricks that I'll share with you, but ultimately you're going to have to come up with your own special hacks...

Hacks that cater to your exact product or service. Hacks that cater to your exact industry and customer base.

But you know your potential customers. You know their habits, their wants and needs. You know what they're looking for so you can figure out a way to get in front of them in a novel way.

If not, then you don't deserve to be selling things to them in the first place, and you don't deserve to get rich off of them.

Remember, business is all about meeting the needs of customers, solving their problems, and adding value.

If you can find a way to do this, the customers will come – and they'll be your biggest evangelists. Tap into that.

Tracking Your Hacks

Before I get into actual Growth Hacking techniques, I want to talk a little bit about tracking and analytics.

It's so very important to track everything you do with your online business, especially when it comes to your marketing.

Luckily, these days it's incredibly cheap and easy to track all of this stuff in great detail.

The first step is adding some sort of analytics tracking to your website. I recommend Google Analytics because it's fairly robust for the cost...which is free.

Google Analytics has a lot of problems, but most of those problems won't affect you (so I'm not even going to discuss them).

It's incredibly easy to integrate Google Analytics into your website, especially if you're using a CMS like Wordpress.

Google will give you a snippet of code to put on your site. That code takes care of everything for you.

You need to put that code snippet on every single page of your website. Leave it off any page, and you won't get data for that page.

Most Wordpress themes have a place where you can paste in that snippet of code just one time. The theme itself will make sure the snippet gets placed on every page of your site.

Google Analytics gives you a ton of information about your website visitors, right out of the box.

You'll see demographic information such as where in the world your visitors are coming from (what country, what state, even what city), and the time of day they visited.

You'll see how they found your site, ie where they came from. Did they find you on Google or click a link on some other website? You'll see exactly.

You'll see if they came from a social media site like Facebook or Twitter or Pinterest or any of the others.

Not only will you see where your visitors live and where they came from, but you'll be able to see exactly what they did on your site; which pages they visited, how long they stayed, the different links on your pages that they clicked on, and more.

You can also easily integrate Google Analytics with your ecommerce system and track how many visitors bought your product or service.

This is great because at one glance you can see that people coming to your site from Facebook tend to purchase more or less than people who come from Twitter or wherever.

If you eventually run Adwords ads, you can integrate them into your Analytics account and track sales based on specific ad clicks.

It's just a wealth of information at your fingertips, and it doesn't cost a penny.

Why is this so important? Well besides the obvious reasons, it's important because it allows you to keep your fingers on the pulse of your Growth Hacking.

Many times, Growth Hacking techniques take on a life of their own. One person tells another, who tells another, who announces it on their email list.

Suddenly you get a flood of orders from people who clicked on that recommendation on that obscure email list.

Normally you'd have no way of ever knowing how those people found you. But with Google Analytics you can figure it out easily and immediately.

Maybe you want to get in touch with that email list owner and offer them a discount for their readers in the future...

Maybe someone tells someone who tells someone who posts about it on some obscure web forum somewhere.

You'll see a flood of visitors from that web forum in your Google Analytics reports.

Maybe you'll want to head over to that forum and answer any questions people might be asking and engage with the community.

A good analytics program allows you to identify where your traffic is coming from so you can focus your efforts on maximizing those situations.

With normal marketing this isn't as important because you sort of know where you traffic is going to come from.

For example, if I plan on spending $100,000 on adword ads this month, I can be fairly sure the traffic coming into my site is from those Google ad clicks.

Sure, I still want to track all that, but it's not as vitally important that I know where my traffic is coming from.

That's the thing that really sets Growth Hacking apart from traditional advertising.

Think of all the commercials on television. Those companies have no idea where their customers are coming from. Maybe someone saw the ad, maybe their friend told them about it, maybe something else.

Those companies have no way of knowing...

We, on the other hand, can *know* where our customers come from. It just takes a little analytics sleuthing.

Plus, analytics help us make our websites and our products better.

If I throw up a sales letter on a web page, and everyone that visits that page leaves within five seconds, I know right away that that sales letter is crap. And since they're leaving so soon, I can guess that it's something right at the top of the sales letter that's putting people off.

So I can test, and tweak, and watch the numbers and see the conversions. I can run split tests (Google Analytics makes that pretty easy to do).

So I can see how people are finding me, how they're interacting with my website, and how to make my site better.

It's just so important.

So make sure you set up Google Analytics as soon as you create your website. There are other analytics packages out there, some free, some costly – with a range in between.

But out of the box, you'll be hard pressed to find anything as easy to use and as robust as Google Analytics.

It's really a no brainer.

Plus there's a huge community behind Google Analytics meaning that you can find tons of tutorials and help setting up and using all of the different features and functions that are available.

Growth Hacking Channels

Before we start talking about the standard basic Growth Hacking techniques, I need to discuss one more thing; Channels.

Growth Hacking is all about word of mouth. The goal is to make your message go viral in whatever way you can.

These days viral word of mouth occurs via social media.

People share on Facebook, Twitter, Pinterest, Instagram, Youtube, SnapChat, and the list of social media networks goes on and on (and increases all the time as the latest new network appears and others decline).

You need to think of each of those Social Media networks as Channels....they are all basically just different paths that your marketing message can stroll down.

You can target each Channel, but you'll never really know which ones will catch fire. These days, social media networks are more integrated than ever. Something that starts out on Instagram can morph into a Tweet that gets shared on Facebook; or any number of different permutations just like that.

What this means for you as a Growth Hacking marketer is that you need to have a presence on as many social media networks as possible.

Sure, you don't have to have a Twitter handle in order for your stuff to go viral on Twitter and the same thing goes for most other Social Media networks.

But having a presence on each network certainly helps. It allows you to participate when something goes viral, it makes it easier for your customers to connect with you where and how THEY want to, it makes it easier to fan the flames when something does catch on.

It's just really important.

So before you start making Growth Hacking moves, be sure to set up accounts and profiles on all the major Social Media networks.

You don't necessarily have to engage in a full blown social media marketing campaign for each network, you really just need to set up an account and set up basic profile pages for your business...just so people can find you when your Growth Hacking stuff starts to work.

Over time you'll create Growth Hacking campaigns geared towards each Social Media network, but when you're just starting out, the important thing is to just create a presence.

Create decent looking profile pages with decent looking images and graphics. You don't have to spend money on this, you can use free templates, but make an effort.

So I've introduced the concept of Growth Hacking to you and explained why Analytics are so vitally important, and discussed Channels. In the next chapter we'll go over some basic standard Growth Hacking techniques to get you started.

CHAPTER EIGHT

* * *

GROWTH HACKING TIPS

Let's dive in and talk about some standard Growth Hacking techniques.

Yes I said that you need to invent your own Growth Hacking strategies to fit your own market and customer base, but there are some basic techniques that most people will be able to use regardless.

These will generally be fairly basic techniques. Some of them might seem like "duh" type things, so bear with me. Even if they're obvious, they still need to be discussed and you never know, you might learn a few things that you didn't already know!

So let's dive in...

Growth Hacking Technique #1
The Social Media Link Circle

So you've set up profile pages on all the major social media sites. Good job. Gold star.

Be sure to list your website domain name somewhere prominent on your profile page. Make it a link if you can (if the site allows you to – most do).

Most social media sites let you put a link to your website, hell most of them have a special place for you to type it in. For the ones that don't, you can hack it so that they do by adding your domain name to the description section of the profile page.

Yes, this seems like an insanely obvious suggestion, but you'd be surprised how many profiles I see with no link to a website; or if there is a link – it's buried somewhere and hard to find or see.

Make sure the link to your website is prominent, obvious, and jumps right out at you.

Use it in the graphics on your profile page, even if those graphics aren't clickable. Get it out there.

That's part one of this hack. Part two is to link to all of your social media accounts on your website. That's the link circle.

But you need to do this differently than most people do.

Most people plaster every page of their website with links to their social media accounts. Many Wordpress themes make this possible by default (you know at the top or bottom of every page you'll see little social media icons).

That's just stupid.

The point of social media is to get people talking about you and ultimately get them to come to your website so that you can sell them something.

The purpose of your website is to sell stuff and make money.

Once someone comes to your website, they are a captive audience!

You've got their attention! Focus that attention on one thing and one thing only...selling them your product.

What you DON'T want is for them to see some link on your website to your other social media accounts, and click on one of those links and leave your site.

Stupid.

So don't put links to your social media accounts on every page of your site...but they need to be on *some* pages.

Which pages? Your "About Us" and/or "Contact Us" pages. That's pretty much it.

Most websites have an "About Us" and a "Contact Us" page and yours should too. THAT's where you put links to every single one of your social media accounts.

Why?

You want to give that information to people who are truly looking for it. There's a difference between someone clicking an "About Us" page because they want to learn about you and discover where your social media accounts are, and someone who's reading your sales letter and gets distracted by the social media buttons.

One if fine, the other is disastrous.

And also, you want to link all of your social media accounts together and claim them in the name of the almighty goddess Google.

No one knows for sure if social media is a factor that Google uses to rank websites, but I feel it in my bones that they do.

So link juice counts. Link to your social media accounts, and have them link back to you. Get Google spinning on a feedback loop between your website and your various social media accounts.

Again, this probably sounds like common sense to you but you'd be surprised how many people are too lazy to do this.

Growth Hacking Technique #2
Teach For Growth

Content Marketing is all the rage these days, and for good reason. If you can produce good content, people will flock to you.

But as a startup, you might not feel that your product or service lends itself to content marketing. After all, if you're just selling a widget of some sort – you might not feel that content marketing lends itself to you.

You're wrong.

It doesn't matter what you are selling, be it product or service; be it exciting or boring – you can still use content marketing in some way.

Typically I find that the teaching method of content marketing can be a great growth hack because if you do a good job, it can be quite shareable.

What do I mean by the teaching method?

The teaching method has two prongs. The first prong is fairly easy to visualize; I call it "product education".

With product education you should aim to create content that explains everything there is to know about your product.

Content should be in the form of videos, white papers, pdf files, slideshare slides, special reports, infographics, and blog posts; and is posted on your website and across all your social media channels.

With product education, your aim is to show customers exactly how to use your product.

If you're selling software, then create screencast videos showing your software in use. Create pdf manuals and white papers describing how to use all the features. Build case studies showing how other customers used it (or *could use it*), etc.

If you're selling a physical product, create videos showing the product, showing it in use, showing everything important a customer might need to know about it.

Educate your customers about your product. Give them the information they need to make a buying decision.

Pretty straight forwards.

The second prong of the teaching method may be a little more tricky. It's the second prong that really lends itself as a growth hack (because let's face it, a product education screenshot video showing your product in use isn't going to get shared all that much).

Let's call the second prong "shareable education".

Shareable education may or may not be about your product directly. Shareable education is geared toward your market and the people in it.

Shareable education is tangential. It relates to your own product or service but the relation doesn't have to be terribly strong.

Ask yourself this question...

"If my customers are interested in my product, what else are they interested in that may be related?"

Or... "how can I tie my product or service into something happening in the news right now?"

The purpose of shareable education is to create content that goes viral.

Infographics are great for this sort of thing, people love to share those on Facebook and Twitter, or to post them on their own blogs.

List-type articles are great for this.

Back in the late 90's I created one of the earliest search engine marketing tools out there and over three million people used it (which was a lot back then).

Today if I was selling SEO software, I'd create lots of shareable list articles like...

"21 Ways To Tweak Your Website's Onpage SEO For Higher Rankings"

"15 Mistakes That Websites Make That Crush Their Google Rankings"

"5 Tips To Boost Your Website Search Rankings in 5 Minutes or Less"

Etc.

They're absolutely related to our product, search engine optimization software, but not directly ABOUT the product.

They are shareable. They're the kind of education pieces that people are hungry for, but also lend themselves to sharing.

I'd package those things up in many different ways. First I'd publish them as a blog post on my website.

I'd also make them into a pdf report that is downloadable (after a person enters their email address).

Then I'd repurpose each of them into an infographic (lists are great as infographics).

Finally I'd create a screencast video for each of them and post them to my blog, as well as Youtube and Facebook/Twitter/etc.

You can boost your Facebook posts for pennies and they'll shoot out to people who are interested in your industry.

For instance, there's a bunch of people on Facebook who identify themselves as being interested in SEO. For a few dollars, I can post my "5 Tips To Boost Your Website Search Rankings in 5 Minutes or Less" post to those people and I'd be willing to bet anything that many of those people will "like" that post, and a fair number of them will share it on their own wall.

Get enough people to do that and your message can go viral very quickly.

Of course, with any sort of shareable education content that you create, you'll need to carefully mention your own product somewhere.

For instance, if I created a blog post titled "5 Tips To Boost Your Website Search Rankings in 5 Minutes or Less", at the bottom of the post I'd put a little blurb about my SEO software. Something like...

"If you enjoyed these 5 tips, check out www.whatever.com to see how our SEO software can drive traffic to your site risk free"

...or something like that.

You need some call to action somewhere within the piece; otherwise it won't matter if the thing goes viral because no one will know your website exists or that you're selling something they may be interested in.

You may or may not want to be subtle about it...it just depends (and you can play around with that).

The point is; shareable education is just that - shareable. Plus it doesn't cost you anything except your time.

You don't even need to reinvent the wheel here, just look and see what sort of things are currently being shared across social media and copy them. Don't copy things exactly, but create similar items.

There are lots of tools out there that show you what's currently popular in the share-o-sphere.

buzzsumo.com is one of my favorites. They offer a free and paid version.

Basically buzzsumo.com allows you to type in a keywords and it will show you what's being shared across various social media networks based on that keyword.

You'll see actual titles of things and how many times they were shared on Facebook, Linkedin, Twitter, Pinterest, and Google+

This is fantastic for many different reasons, but mostly because it shows you what people are interested in sharing related to your specific industry.

You don't have to guess...just see what's popular and try to mimic them.

Buzzsumo.com also has a trending feature across certain set top level categories (like tech, health, news, sports, etc).

That's not as helpful to you because it's too broad...but still helpful because it lets you keep your finger on the pulse of current events.

Finding some way to tie your product or service into current events can be powerful from a sharing point of view.

Finally, buzzsumo.com has an "influencers" feature that allows you to find people who blog, post, tweet, or whatever within your industry based on their Twitter profiles.

You'll see their website URL, how many followers they have, their reply and re-Tweet ratios, and more.

This is a great way to find people to reach out to. If you can get some of those people to share your stuff, it makes it much easier for your stuff to go viral.

You can use BuzzSumo.com for free, but you'll get hit with a daily limit that only allows you a few searches per day and restricts the amount of info you get.

Upgraded plans start at around $99 a month, which seems pretty expensive. In fact, that's really the most expensive item we've discussed in the Smart Startup method.

In my opinion, it's totally worth the expense because the information you'll glean from this tool can make or break your business.

One piece of viral content can bring in hundreds or thousands of dollars in sales to your product.

Without the info that you'll get from BuzzSumo or some other similar service; you're really just throwing darts at a board blind folded.

BuzzSumo allows you to take the blindfold off. Sure you're still throwing darts at a board (you never really know which of your pieces of content will take off and go viral), but at least now you stand a sporting chance!

And really, a hundred bucks isn't that bad. You certainly don't need to raise Venture Capital money to be able to afford the service for a month or two.

Finally, check out the BuzzSumo blog for tons of tips and ideas on creating great viral content pieces; http://buzzsumo.com/blog

Growth Hacking Technique #3
PR Growth Hacking

PR, of course, stands for Press Release and is a pretty standard practice for big companies.

Whenever they have a new product or service or an announcement of any kind, big companies will issue a press release.

If the company is important enough, or big enough, any number of press outlets will probably pick it up.

PR is a lot harder for small companies, especially small companies with little to no track record.

It's also fairly expensive to blast out a press release to the broad world. Coupled with the fact that it might not be effective in any way shape or form; PR marketing tends to be pretty far down the list for smaller companies.

Fortunately, a Smart Startup can hack the PR world fairly easily.

Why?

Because your Smart Startup is all about a Big Idea.

Big Ideas are much easier to get picked up by the press than regular ideas (or even "good" ideas).

Big Ideas have a hook...they have something that catches the attention and the imagination of people. That's why they're big.

The PR Growth Hack is different than just blasting out a press release and hoping it gets picked up.

With a Smart Startup PR hack, you need to focus on finding media outlets that are specifically tailored to your product or industry. Believe me, they're out there.

For instance, if I was selling some sort of techy product or service, I'd focus on the website HackerNews.

That site is directly related to my industry, getting noticed there can instantly send thousands of people to your website.

The trick is to not release a boring old press release, but make it interesting; make it read like an article with a headline that grabs attention.

Tailor your release to the media that you're targeting.

Make it shareable, make it interesting, give it a hook.

Luckily your Big Idea inherently has all of those things built into it already...so this should be easy.

Don't just focus on targeting media outlets, focus on influencers as well (like the influencers you discover using Buzz Sumo).

Compile a list of them and start contacting them. Start dialogs. Give them exclusive interviews. Help THEM create content that they can pass along to their users.

It's not about you telling your story to get good press...it's about you helping those influencers create compelling content that they can feed to their email lists, their fans, their followers, etc.

Give an influencer something unique that their readers can't find anywhere else and everybody wins.

With a little legwork, this can boost your site traffic instantly and doesn't cost you a thing to do.

It's just a matter of research. Head over to Google and start searching for Blogs in your industry. Find *magazines* in your industry. Find *newsletters* in your industry. Find *influencers* in your industry.

Start to compile a spreadsheet of the media and the contact information for your contact point.

Once you've compiled a list of a few hundred names, just start contacting them.

Start with email.

If that doesn't work, reach out on social media.

If that doesn't work, pick up the phone and call them.

Maybe only one in ten will respond, and maybe only one in ten of those will eventually run your PR content.

That's ok, it only takes a handful of these contacts to take off in order to start the viral ball rolling.

Conclusion

I've given you three basic Growth Hacking techniques in this chapter.

Maybe you wanted more, but the three that I gave you (especially the last two) are meaty enough for you to spend all your time working on.

Sure, there are many other Growth Hacking techniques out there, but the ones I gave you in this chapter will put you well on the path to Smart Startup success.

And don't forget; you really need to invent your own Hacks anyway.

Spend time thinking about your market and how you can reach people in clever ways.

It's that one clever growth hack that no one else is using but you (because you invented it) that's going to really pay off in the long run.

Part of the fun of building your own business is coming up with novel ways to pull in customers.

If there was a manual that listed the 20 exact steps you need to take with your marketing, then everyone would do it and everyone would be rich.

You need to think for yourself, think outside of the box, and think viral.

Once you learn to come up with these things on your own, then you'll become truly dangerous...

CHAPTER NINE

* * *

SUMMING UP

Well, you've made it to the end of the book!

That's all there is to it! Are you disappointed that the Smart Startup method isn't more complicated?

Part of the beauty of this system is that it's so simple.

Come up with your Big Idea, build a simple Wordpress website to get your proof of concept up and running, get the word out through Social Media and PR growth marketing - primarily by creating shareable educational content...then sit back and see what your customers tell you!

That's it!

I hope you enjoyed the book, and I hope you got a lot out of it. I had a good time writing it.

I hope to see you over at StartupFool.com

The purpose of that website is to create a place for people like us to hang out and learn from each other.

I try to blog there every day, sharing tips and tricks that Smart Startup types can use to help grow their business.

Head over and say hi, ask me questions, read some tutorials.

Watch a video course or two. It's good times, I tell ya!

Can I Ask You A Quick Favor?

If you enjoyed this book, would you help me out real quick?

Reviews at Amazon literally make or break a book. Just a handful of reviews can vault a book up the best-seller rankings...it's especially important for authors like me who don't have major publishing houses behind them.

If you'd take just a minute or two and head back to Amazon **here**:

www.startupfool.com/smart

That will redirect to the book's Amazon page where you can leave a quick review...I'd really appreciate it!

Then head over to StartupFool.com and let me know, I'll give you a little something for your efforts ;-)

Thanks again for reading this book, I'd love to hear about your Smart Startup successes! Good luck!

THE END

All material contained in this book is for informational purposes only and is no substitute for professional advice. Neither John Elder, StartupFool.com or it's affiliates (collectively referred to as COMPANY) make any guarantees of the tactics or strategies described in this book. Successful use of any tactic or strategy described in this book depends on the specific person, their experience, and their business and marketing ability. COMPANY makes no claims or guarantees regarding income generated from the use of any tactic or strategy described in this book. Reader agrees to indemnify and hold COMPANY harmless from and against any and all claims, demands, liabilities, expenses, losses, damages, attorney fees arising from any and all claims and lawsuits for libel, slander, copyright, and trademark violation as well as all other claims resulting from reading this book.

John Elder

www.ingramcontent.com/pod-product-compliance
Lightning Source LLC
Chambersburg PA
CBHW031808190326
41518CB00006B/250